Forever Etched In Me

S.SUNDQUIST

S.Sundquist

This book is dedicated to a rock climber:
You showed me how to fall in love with life
and gave me my first taste of freedom,
as well as peace.
Both of which led my ink stained heart
to the mountains within yours.
Thank you my love, for being my muse.
I wish you everything your heart desires and
then some;

"Never go in search of love, go in search of life,
and life will find you the love you seek."
- Atticus

Teenagers

We drink,
we do drugs,
and fall madly in love;
but don't you know
that this is all a show.
We're hurting inside
and can't let it go.
If you follow
our love will grow.
Maybe it's because someone died today,
or even yesterday.
Maybe it's because someone is starving today,
or was put in prison
for the wrong reasons yesterday.
Our parents tell us,
"You're just young you don't know anything"
Oh don't you know
we know more than you,
with the shit that we've been through.

Gen Z

This is our generation.
The rules that the people of before have set,
have worn us down
and made us tired.
The old ways must be changed.
Try and come at us.
We dare you.
Because we are young
you act as if this is a game
and you'll surely win.
I assure you,
we're not playing.
We are here.
Here to forever change it all.

As We Fall

Can you not see them falling?
Falling off the edge of oblivion.
Can you see their anger hiding
behind the flames and their tears
washed away by the rain?
Where do we go from here?
Oh, can't you see us?
Can you not see us falling?
You hate what you don't know.
Oh honey, come and join the show.
You can fall along with us, but you say
"I'm scared to fall."
What you don't know
is that we have parachutes
on our backs and you would've known,
if you had given the lost a chance.

First Love

I didn't comprehend it then
but you, dad, were terrified of me.
Scared of a six-year old little girl.
You were terrified of my voice.
You were the first love of my life.
Or at least you were supposed to be,
but love doesn't treat you
the way you treated me.
You silenced me.
Even though you were gone
I continued in silence.
My voice is raw and pure
because I've never used it.
You let me be there,
but then became afraid I'd tell what I saw.
I lost my voice.
I didn't know it was okay to speak.
I searched for you in many ways
trying to replace the hole you left,
but that hole can only be filled by me.
By a little girl who lost her way and her voice.

Beginning

She didn't know if she wanted to fly
or stay grounded.
She didn't know how her life would turn out.
Yet, she knew one thing.
She knew that she wanted someone
to inspire her,
before she fell in love with them.
So she waited and she waited.
Until one day,
she met a boy behind a grocery store .
The stars in their eyes knew that they were it.
Because as the two of them
looked at each other that first time,
they smiled because they knew.

New Love

Maybe it's the way you laugh,
or the way you smile.
Maybe it's how you look at me,
or the way you see the world.
It might just be how special you make me feel.
Maybe it's the way you touch me,
or how we kiss.
Maybe it's how you give me butterflies,
or how stupidly happy you make me.
It might just be how you electrify me.
Maybe it's how much I miss you
when you're gone,
or the sound of your voice.
Maybe it's all of these and more,
one thing's for sure
I might just be falling in love with you.

Carnival

As the sun sets, all the colorful lights turn on
and that's when the magic sets in.
All the people are enjoying their own
bewitchment.
All busy in their own little worlds.
Then there's us.
You're trying to calm me,
as I desperately try to be brave for you.
We reach the end of the line
and you somehow get me on the ferris wheel.
I'm still so terrified,
but your eyes lock onto mine and you say,
"I'll be right next to you, you'll be okay."
I hold onto you like my life depends on it.
You laugh and hold onto me just the same.
The view is great,
and so are you.

Feelings You Brought

I know that we are meant to be.
Maybe not forever,
but right now is all I need.
At the moment, that's good enough for me.
Before you came into my life,
my world lost its pigment
and suddenly you showed me it
through your eyes.
You brought peace to my mind,
fire to my heart,
and freedom to my soul.

Thai Food

There's a small restaurant in the city,
hidden amongst all the others.
We were dressed in our best,
and others stared at us as to why.
The smells of the spices enriched our nostrils.
It was so loud we could barely hear each other,
odd because there weren't many people there.
When we tasted the pad thai and curry,
we fell in love
with that little restaurant on Center St.
We walked to a stop light that night,
where people whistled and clapped
at us in their cars.
We laughed and kissed there.
You took me to my first school dance then,
even though I have two left feet.
It was so loud we could barely
hear each other over the music,
but somehow our bodies knew what to do.
Everyone there danced the same, except for us.
It was the kind of dancing you see in movies.
You dipped me low with your hands on my waist
and looked into my eyes and smiled.
It was like everything in the room stopped,
and it was just us.
You, me, and the magic in between.
It wasn't the night we had imagined,
it was better.

Rock Climbing

Up, up, up.
Use your strength.
Put the white chalk on your fingertips.
Hold the solid rock in front of you.
Use your strength
and climb.
Go up, up, up.
Look below and imagine the fall.
Fear bubbles into your chest and you panic.
You freeze.
Then you hear his voice
"You're okay, I got you."
You relax and look towards the sky,
it's bright and blue.
The buzz of the world disappears,
the lights dim out,
nature sings,
and the sun shines.
The cold rock in front of you
is begging you
to climb it.
To reach the top and touch the clouds.
You climb.
Up, up, up.
You use the strength and reassurance he gives
to touch the puffy white pillows in the sky.
Your fear subsides
because you trust him with your life.
As you begin to reach the top

you stop and realize,
this is the closest you'll ever be to paradise.

Find Each Other in One Another

There are times he tastes like honey
other times he tastes like fresh air.
Both so soft and sweet.
It's savoring and intoxicating.
There are times he trails his hands
along my body,
and times he quickly pulls me closer.
Both leave electricity throughout me.
There are times he'll get me to face my fears,
and times he'll protect me from them.
He shields me from harm and brightens my day.
He takes me higher than the mountain tops
and anchors me to the earth.
He got lost in the swirl of
my dark chocolate eyes
and I in the currents of his.
Being lost in him,
being lost in me,
isn't being lost at all.
It's more like being found.

Ants

How many are there?
People I mean.
We don't know.
Because people are being born
and dying every day.
Sitting up here on one of the peaks of the earth,
above all the noise and lights
with no one and nothing,
but you and I.
Looking down at all those little dots flickering.
Moving, moving, moving.
Not stopping for even a moment.
All the houses and buildings look like a grid.
We can see all the cars and anything that moves.
We're above, looking down at everyone.
I realize all these little people are their own,
and that we look like an ant farm of many.

Home is Where You Are

The shadows cover us like a blanket
with the tv on in the background,
he looks into my chocolate eyes
and I in the waves of his.
He holds me,
as if to protect me from any and all harm.
I cling to him,
to reassure that I am always there.
He whispers to me,
"You are my home."
and he is mine.

The Color Hidden in the Black and White

When you opened up my eyes
I saw a different kind of light.
All these colors swarming around me
like I'm in the eye of a rainbow hurricane.
I feel like time has stopped
when your eyes look into mine.
You surround me with your glow,
a magnificent mix of color,
all combined into one person.
You're the rainbow to my hurricane,
that leads me out of the chaos and darkness
to find peace, light, and love.

Future

Maybe it was the first time,
or the last time,
but somewhere along the line
I fell in love with you.
I don't know what year it is
or where we are,
but I sure hope we're in each others arms.
Looking up at the sky,
laughing as time and clouds pass by.

Lost and Then Found

Forever lost in the void; alone.
There's always a light in the distance,
but no matter how fast or far he runs
he can never catch the brightness.
He's been running for so long.
He seems to have lost himself in the darkness.
For once he comes to a stop in his tracks.
He breathes in and out with his eyes shut,
he feels cold hands grab at his feet and arms,
he doesn't seem to have the strength to fight.
The ground transforms into water, he's sinking.
He tries to scream as he sees the light.
The dark water is almost above his head.
He tears his arms away from the hands,
he raises them in the air trying to stay afloat.
The light after all this time
seems to move closer,
and closer,
and closer.
Until it's right in front of him.
It's a flashlight,
being held by a girl.
She pulls him out of the water,
but doesn't let him go.
The girl says,
"I've been running up and down this void
forever; alone.
Always trying to reach the golden light,
which I now know was your hair."

Holiday Love

Throughout the seasons,
the holidays,
the events,
throughout the color
and black and white of our lives
I've found you.
I've f
     a
      l
       l
        e
         n
           for you.
You've become:
the pixels to my picture,
the words to my poetry,
the Tim Tams to my hot chocolate,
and the love of my life.

Lucky

He kisses me,
as if I'm air and he's struggling to breathe.
He holds me,
as if I'm gravity and he'll float away
at any minute.
He listens to me,
as if I'm the only person alive
and he craves the sound beyond the silence.
He talks to me,
as if we're martians and we're the only ones
who speak the same language.
He misses me,
as if I'm the sky and he's the sea
giving me my vibrant blue clothes.
He loves me,
as if I'm the moon and he's the sun.
He looks at me,
as if he's known me forever.
"I see you."

My Muse

I admire the strength your heart holds
and the wisdom of your mind.
You, my love,
are a wild and honest soul.
It's rare to find that these days.
What was once the colorless pixels of my life
have become vibrant sweeps of color.
You taught me to live for myself
and to look at how beautiful the world is,
even in the darkness.
You've taught me fearlessness and bravery.
You have made me feel alive.
I admire the freedom beneath your eyes.
You are my inspiration.

In Love With a Bad Boy

I was never
infatuated with bad boys before.
Not until him.
He's the type of man
who's tall, dark, and handsome.
The kind whose smile
is so beautiful it could save the world.
Who smokes blunts
while soaking in sunsets.
The kind that makes you look
at the smallest parts of life
and see entire universes hidden there.
The kind that makes you love him
to the end of everything and on.

Fifth Sense

and yet;
you cherish me and my flaws,
you hold me tightly through the storm,
you protect me,
you caress my face in your palms,
you kiss me as if it'll be your last.
Every touch is electrifying.
Everywhere your fingers linger upon
I still feel when they're gone.
Everytime you touch me,
it feels like your touching me
for the very first time.

Home

I always thought that I fell.
I always thought that I was still falling.
I thought that I fell for you,
but I was wrong.
I saw you as if I already knew you.
I saw something real,
something handsome in every way.
I saw you as something that lasts,
something to love.
I had felt misunderstood
and out of place for so long,
that when I found you
I was dumbfounded.
It was as if I walked into a house
only to realize I had found my home.

Part of a Letter For a Deceased Father

I looked for love in all the wrong ways,
trying to replace your space.
Over time my heart turned to stone,
then I met a man that turned it to gold.
The space he takes in my heart
is nothing like a father's place,
but you have to understand
that I never had a man
to show me what real love was.
I never had a chance.
I learned how to love better than you.
I now have the knowledge
that if a real man loves you he'll build you up,
and stick around to fight.
He'll help you find the truth.
It's a fairytale for me,
something I'm not used to.
All I wanted was to be your princess,
but I'm happy that I'm his.
I wish you could see
what your little girl turned out to be.

Sight

My butterfly stained vision
guides me toward you in the night.
Won't you be my light?
So that I may once again
open my eyes to you.

Find

Touch me with your eyes,
before your hands.
Touch me with your hands,
before your lips.
Place every inch of you inside me,
I want all of you.
Touch me with your lips,
before your heart.
Touch me and come.
Come find your home within me.

When We First Met

I met you behind a grocery store.
Thought we could have some fun,
thought it was going to be a hit and run,
going to be a kum and go.
Didn't know we were going
to want something more,
that you were going to be my ride or die,
that you were going to stay by my side,
that you were going to inspire me,
that you were going to be stuck in my mind,
that you were going to love me.
Falling for you was like coming home.
You give me butterflies,
but also calm the chaos inside.
You start the embers of my heart
until it turns into a fire.
You became my best friend so quick.
It took us awhile to open up,
but when we did we just clicked.
Thought we could have some fun,
thought it was going to be a hit and run,
going to be a kum and go.
We grow together.
Thick and thin together.
We're young and wild.
From ramen to frozen burritos,
you became the love of my life.

Significant Other

Look at me,
like the sun looks at the solar system.
Protect me,
like a clam protects its pearl.
Hold me close,
like the air in your lungs.
Kiss me,
like a rainbow after a storm.
Make love to me,
like the sun makes love to the moon.
Love me,
like I'm half of you.
As you are half of me.

My Love

I don't tremble.

I don't fall.

I was scared for so long,

but you, my love,

you've gotten me falling on my knees for you.

I tremble in your light.

I've fallen for you

and that doesn't scare me at all.

You are the only one

I'll ever be on my knees for.

Wings

I blocked out the sun,
but there you were
with your golden hair
guiding me toward the light.
Those ocean eyes
I can't help but stare deeply into.
Never looking away.
You got these wings of mine
flapping in the sunlight.
Ready to take flight.

Deserving

I've been writing about you.
To the point my fingers
are covered with my words.
You once said you didn't deserve me,
but you're wrong.
The only man who deserves me
is the one who thinks he doesn't.
Because you know my true worth.
You my dear,
have earned the ink stained heart of a poet
and I will continue
to write you into infinity

Favorite

As a child we choose our favorite colors.
We also choose our favorite foods,
when no matter how much we eat it
it still tastes so good.
I'm craving ramen and frozen burritos.
You became my favorite color.
You became my light.
You became the inspiration
I never knew I needed.
In the infiniteness of it all you are my muse.
As children we also have a favorite person,
mine is you.

Remembrance

Walking down memory lane can be full of pain
or it can bring you joy.
I remember our beginning;
how young you looked,
how your smile caught my eye,
how you were so in love with life.
You inspired me.
I remember the brisk night air,
finding its way in between our bodies
as we made love under the moonlight.
I remember before
when we were only friends.
Now, almost a year later
we catch each other's eye even still.

Struggle of Ours

I've lost my words.
I don't know what to say.
All I can do is hope we'll be okay.
Maybe tomorrow
the sun will come out of hiding
and shine back on us,
but who knows.
I've lost my words.

Come Back

I'm supposed to be the one
to hold you down
and fly you up,
but baby you're too high now.
You've exceeded the clouds
and into the stars.
You've been in outer space
way too long for my taste.
Please.
Come back home.
I miss you.

If I Could Take Back the Words

I wonder if you really cared for me
as much as I did you.
I ask myself if there were any signs
that I missed that you were going to do this.
How did I not see that you were going to leave?
I hate that you broke my heart,
I hate that you broke me.
I was so caught up in my pain,
that I said some words that I didn't mean.

"I hate you."

Now I'm on my knees
begging you to forgive me.
I'd do anything to take back those three words.
They haunt me
as everyday gets colder and colder.
I lost control of my temper and my pain.
I hate the heartache and the heartbreak,
but oh, my love, I could never hate you.
Not ever.

Distance

Eight hundred thirty two miles,
that's the distance between us.
Despite that,
you've never left my thoughts or my heart.
Memories of us constantly flood my mind
on a continuous loop.
It's like a never ending trip.
I used to think I was an addict,
that you were my drug
and I was going through withdrawal.
However, I've come to the realization
that you weren't my drug.
Because you were the one to clear my head.
Oh honey, soon those miles will be inches
and we'll see each other again.
Once more I am hit with this longing.
I find myself at two am,
lonely and missing you.
I also find myself at two pm,
busy and missing you even more.
I'll be here,
when time and distance is no longer against us
and when you're ready for us.

Fourth of July

Just another day
filled with thinking about you is ending.
Only to be met with tomorrow
and the returning thoughts of yesterday.
Thinking.
Hurting.
Dreaming.
Hoping.
Part of me wants it to stop,
but it's all I have left of you.
That and our memories.
I won't give it up.
People want someone new
to watch the lights in the sky with.
Where as I,
just want to be back home,
with you.

As I've Bloomed

I've been running around the clock,
working on myself.
Now I've made my way back home.
I had wilted
and now I've bloomed.
Here I stand,
frozen in place,
staring at you.
Is it possible you got even more beautiful?
Can a man be beautiful? I ask myself
The ocean blue of your eyes say yes.
The carcasses of my butterflies
flutter upon the sight of you.
My hummingbird heart,
beats like it never has for anyone else.
The ashes of my heart,
catch aflame once more.
As I've bloomed,
I've found myself.
However, just like you did before
you make me want to reach for more.

Our Love in The Sky pt 1

There's something about the way he is,
something about the way he lives.
Something about him
has always been able to get under my skin.
Under the sun and the moon
we've found what had been lost,
our hidden treasure amidst the stars.
They told us,
that if we found each other once more
our treasure would again find us.
I suppose the stars are never wrong.
Unless instead of fireflies
they're giant balls of gas.
I want to say I've fallen for you again,
but how can I fall once more,
if I never got up to begin with?

You Were and Still are Everything

I may be smaller than you,
but it's okay to collapse into my arms.
You are such a strong person,
but you don't have to be with me.
You don't always have to fight.
I too might not be okay,
but I am forever here for you.
No matter what,
I'll have your back.
Your enemies become my enemies,
and I will protect you.

The Beauty of You

Here you lay,
not quite asleep and not quite awake.
Your mind filled with racing thoughts
of your past, present, and future.
Some say you're lost,
I disagree.
Because I see you,
where they don't.
Because you're laying on me asleep,
curled up into a ball like a child.
You are so striking in this moment.
The rawness of you is breathtaking.
As I soothe you;
I see you for the boy you were,
the man you are,
and the man you will one day be.
You will rise against the odds
people have put against you.
Here you lay, asleep and dreaming.
I smile
as I brush your sunkissed hair from your face
and think to myself,
"You're really going to be something one day,
you're going to go places my love."

I Miss You

I miss the little things.
Like how your smile would form on your face
making me want to kiss it,
how your hands felt on my skin,
the sweetness of your lips on mine,
the softness of your body
colliding with my own,
the way you would concentrate
when trying to make something your very best.
I miss your warmth,
days filled with Netflix and ramen,
nights with you driving and laughing,
days spent with you falling asleep,
the security and safety of your arms,
how I'd hold and care for you
in your times of need.
I miss everything.
I miss the good and the bad
and everything in between.
I just miss you.
All of you.

Our Love in The Sky pt 2

We may no longer be together,
but our love is still forever.
It's not lost,
only floating in the stars,
waiting for us to return to each other.
So it can return to us.
Even if our love never comes back down
from that never ending sky.
I will love you,
for eternity and on.

Giants in The Sky

When I say,

"I miss mountains."

what I really mean is,

"I miss you."

You taught me to climb,

you showed me the beauty,

you got me to face my fear.

I miss the height,

the thrill,

the tranquility.

I miss your eyes,

your laugh,

the way you carry yourself,

your presence,

you.

So think of me,

when you see those giants in the sky.

Because I think of you,

every time I miss them.

Which just so happens to be all the time.

My Promise to You

I'm scared that you'll forget.
Forget us.
Forget me.
I will always be here.
I will always listen.
You'll never be alone with me.
It's you and me.
In four months,
a year from now,
ten,
fifty.
This is an infinite promise I'm making to you.
"To always be there for you
whenever you need me."

Blooming Flowers

In order to bloom
you have to break,
you have to fall off a cliff,
you have to let yourself shatter
into a million pieces.
Let yourself drown in the ocean of your tears,
let yourself run free,
and allow yourself to feel the pain.
That's the only way to grow.
It's the only way to bloom.

Infinite

There are billions of people in the world.
I'm young with the world at my fingertips
even though they're covered in paint.
I know that out of all those people I could
find someone that could make me happy,
that could love me.
but no one can love me
as much or as passionate as you,
I could never love anyone
with magic other than you.
You've turned my stone cold heart
into gold and have set it aflame.
Ever since we found each other
you've been my constant inspiration.

Priorities

I don't expect or want
to be thought about every second of the day.
You need to be happy on your own
before you can be jubilant with me.
In the end
I hope it'll be you and me,
loving wildly
and saying goodnight instead of goodbye.
When we are slightly older
and our minds less hectic,
if you'll be right for me
and I'll be right for you.
Until then,
we'll live and patiently wait.

The Only One

I'm not down for just anyone,
only you.
I'll never leave your side.
No matter the distance,
we'll both be looking
at the same moon and stars.
That's a little bit closer to each other.
No matter the time,
no matter the distance,
I'll always be right next to you.

Victim and Victor

"What flows flows, what crashes crashes."
"What is meant for you will happen."
"You can either be victim or victor."
Bullshit.
I'm tired of everyone
telling me I can't or I won't.
Come at me with your negativity
I'll come at you with a bat.
Wanting and wishing isn't enough.
You have to hustle
and take it day by day.
You have to work to get what you want.
You'll cry for what you lost
and what you never got,
but did you fight
and work for what you want?
You are a victim,
but also a victor.
If you don't fight for what you want,
don't waste your tears for what you lost.

Take a Chance

I don't want to play games,
but I will not stay confined either.
I will wait for you,
but I'm over the excuses.
We messed up,
to the point that our hearts broke.
but what will you get by being stuck in the past?
Why won't you take a chance?
What will you lose if you just take my hand?
Your lips taste like nicotine,
so kiss me.
Look into my eyes,
and say you'll fight for us day by day.
Because that's what I'm doing.
Fighting for you.

Let Me Be the One Who Saves You

My heart begins to beat
as fast as a two second ad.
No longer shy to say the words.
There's so much to say
and so little time.
How can I make you believe?
There's so many things I want to tell you.
So many things I have yet to say.
If you are ever in need
I'll be instantly at your rescue.
Forever there for you.
Even if we're not together,
you'll always have my heart.

Another Farwell

There's magic in this world.
In laying here with you watching our shows,
in reading my words to you,
in climbing the giants in the sky,
in looking into your ocean eyes.
It's the same magic
the sun and the moon feel when they kiss,
that turns pumpkins into carriages,
and that wakes a sleeping castle.
There's magic
in little diners where we went back in time,
in dancing under the lights
as you carried me like a princess,
in seeing each other across an intersection
as I jump into your arms,
in all the moments
when were the only ones in the universe.
That's the kind of magic you see in movies
and hear about in fairytales.
It's your hummingbird heartbeat,
as we say goodbye
once more.

Seperation

We've been apart for awhile now,
but we've ventured to the stars
and have shared our bond once again.
Oh that meant the world to me.
It hurts me
the way I hurt you.
It's easier to breathe now
after we reconnected.
They say I should let you go.
They say it would help me,
but I think about you
and your smile and dreams.
I came to the conclusion
that you could hate me,
you can never forgive me,
but I will never give up on you.
Just as love will not give up on us.

Closer to More

For so long I've been telling you
the way you make me feel,
but as the sun set and the moon rose,
as our lives go on,
as we stare into the void that is our distance
I'd rather show you.
After all of my words
I want to prove my love and admiration to you.

Just One More Time

I long for you.
I miss you so much.
I keep thinking to myself
if I just had one more nap,
one more meal,
one more drive,
one more kiss,
one more hug.
If when I said goodbye
I held you longer and tighter,
then maybe I'd be okay.
but no matter how hard I kiss you
or how long I hold you
I'll always want more time.
I want you,
one more time.
Next time however,
I intend to keep you.
So until then,
I will wait and miss you.

The Best of Me

In all my years of pain
tears never fell from my eyes.
I cried, but the rivers never ran.
Then you came along and you made me feel,
everything.
We messed up and we can't take it back.
If I could I would without hesitation.
Knowing I caused you pain eats at me inside.
Every. Single. Second.
The words "I'm sorry" can never be said enough
to explain how sorry I truly am.
If I could take away all your pain I would.
The oceans keep roaring now.
The waves, always splashing down my cheek.
I'm clinging to the hope of,
"One day and as you wish"
I imagine you:
sunkissed hair, childish smile,
and dreaming eyes.
Oh my sunshine, you have no idea
how much I miss you, not a clue.
No one can understand how every single
part of me misses every single part of you.
You are the very best of me.

The Things We Want

You have caution tape around your heart now.
Even though I'm the reason it's there,
I'm also the one who can remove it.
Men have emotions and feelings
just as women do.
Women want to be treated as queens,
men as kings.
It's fifty fifty.
I know what I want and I know you know too.
The question is, what do you want?
Ti amo.

Forever and Always You

I was once your first choice.
Maybe I still am.
I don't know,
but you're still and will always be,
my first choice.
Your name is like honey dripping from my lips.
It tastes like peace and peaches,
soft and sweet.
The memory of your presence
surrounds me like air,
forcing me to breathe and to wake up everyday.
You never leave my mind.
I can't go a day without thinking about you.
Just like the sun can't go a day without setting,
to let the moon rise.

Owner of My Heart

The pain tangles itself throughout my body,
covering my legs,
interlacing itself in my ribcage,
reaching across my arms and face.
There's a large hole where my heart used to rest.
It's gone, forever residing by yours.
You took my heart with you,
and I'm not asking for it back.
I want you, thief of my heart, to have it.
It belongs to you.
I only wish you didn't take yours from me,
when you left.

Nightmare

The color and light behind my eyes
dim into nothing.
My smile and laugh disappear.
I run as fast as I can through the rain.
Cars zoom past and the droplets hide my tears,
I'm soaked and my makeup is dripping.
I press my palm to my chest
to feel my heartbeat.
There it goes; thump, thump, thump.
Strange, because I know for a fact
that there is no heart hiding there.
It's a void that was once full, now empty.
Here I stand in the storm,
hand pressed to where my heart was.
I close my eyes,
thinking if I wish hard enough
when I open them,
the world will still be layers of thick color.
However, as I do my wish doesn't come true.
As I once again,
am encased in a world of black and white.

Don't Let This Be True

Please tell me that this is a dream.
That we're asleep, holding each other,
and we're in the middle of a nightmare.
Don't tell me this is real.
Don't tell me that I loved and lost you.
You're my epic love, the love of my life.
Tell me that when I wake from this horror
that you'll be holding me tight,
and keeping me safe.
Don't let this be real.

Texts

Rereading old messages
causes the deceased butterflies
in my lungs, to flutter.
Looking at our old photos
causes my heart to beat,
the way it does for only you.
Confusion eats at me
tearing me limb from limb,
causing waves to flow from my eyes.
I laugh as I cry.
Remembering.

Haunt

Are you a ghost?
Because I think of you
everywhere I go,
in everything I do.
Am I your ghost?
Do I cross your mind from time to time
like you do mine?
I think about you always.
I suppose that would make me my own ghost,
haunting the memories I love the most.

Since the Last Time

We've changed.
When I saw you it was like I didn't know you.
I see us in photos
and ask myself why we didn't try.
I wanted to, did you?
It wasn't supposed to be like this.
We were never meant to say goodbye.
You were my best friend,
my love for you is to the end.
Things didn't work out this time,
but let's give us another try?

Days Spent Without You
It's been really difficult
to live without you these days.
Around this time last year,
we were laying on a couch watching our shows.
I wish we could go back to that.
I wish you'd come back to me.
How can I make you see,
that you are the only one for me?
These days without you haunt me.
We had plans.
We had dreams.
Do you know how hard it is to be without you?
What can I do to make you believe?
I'm on my knees begging for you to see me baby.
I miss you.

She Can Never Love You Like I Do

It won't last,
but you're with her now.
Your heart is still wrapped up in caution tape.
She hasn't begun to reach
the ooey gooey center of your love.
She barely scratches the surface.
Where as I am forever etched into it.
I broke your heart, as you did mine.
Yet, here I stand willing to fight.
I'm still here,
even though my heart is in shambles.
I can remove that caution tape
suffocating your heart,
and you can melt the metal
that's scorching mine.
If only you let me.
I can make that organ glow,
even brighter than I did before.
If only you let me.

Last Time I Saw You

Just because our last moment was magic
doesn't mean I wish that to be our last moment.
My thoughts go back to that moment
and break apart.
I break apart.
I miss you so.
If I had known that was going to be our last kiss,
I would have held on a little longer.

Unprepared

My father taught me how to be alone,
and I learned my lesson through his absence.
Despite his and many people's
lack of attendance
none of the pain that they brought,
could ever prepare me for this.
For being alone, without you.
There's so much agony in my heart.
I'm at the edge of this cliff now,
walking a fine line from crashing.
I'm struggling to hold on
and to keep my head up.

Rest in Paradise Z.R

Maybe humans are just animals that live and die.
Maybe our lives really are just dust to the wind.
Or;
Maybe there's a paradise after death.
Maybe our story isn't one of many,
but one story.
I hope a paradise exists.
If it does, that's where I *know* you are.
It seems unreal to have you gone.
but I know that you were a bird,
and it was your time to fly into the sunrise.
A boy so young, so full of life, so full of light.
An angel.
An angel is what we lost that day.
Until we each fly into that sunrise
you'll never be forgotten
by the ones you left behind.

- Happy Birthday

Bound by Love

I've been saying I'm okay.
Hell I thought I was.
I let you go, completely out of love.
I've been avoiding it,
because inside I know the truth.
I don't want it to be.
Oh fuck what will I do?
The truth won't set me free.
I am bound in chains,
with rivers pouring down my face.
Waters - seen by no one other than you.
What would you do if you knew?
The truth has been clear all this time,
but I can't have it.
Oh but I wish I could.

Your Heartbreak

You don't deserve this pain.
You deserve butterflies and flowers.
Someone may one day give those to you,
but don't forget to give them to yourself first.
Find the light beneath the cracks of your heart.
Tear down your concrete walls
and invite the world in.
Find peace in your life.
Fall in love with you,
just as I fell in love with you.

You Saw Beauty In Me

You saw beauty in dirt and nothingness.
You transformed it.
Transformed me into a flower,
into something beautiful.
You are still my continuous sunshine.
I miss you more than you can ever imagine.
I hope one day you'll come find me.
When you do I'll run into your embrace,
and kiss you in a way I never have before.
Because our last kiss I hope against hope,
was not our last.

April 22nd Reminds Me of You
There was a moment, a magical moment.
When I met you,
for the first time.
It was when I first saw you.
I was in awe.
You took my breath away,
and despite the distance you still do.
Everyday.

Halfway There

I remember seeing a universe
within your eyes,
tasting peaches on your lips,
and watching the memoir of the giants
in the sky on your bronze skin.

Let Me

I know I wasn't the first person
to kiss your lips or down your body.
I know that in some places I was only retracing
some of the lines that had already been drawn.
Your scent had been inhaled
by a few before me, and a few after me.
but I know that there was something different
in the way we both felt,
when I kissed your secret places
and you kissed mine.
I know there's magic here,
and it's not only in you and I,
but in the very entity of our love.
I wasn't your first,
but I hope that I can be your last.

Real

If we were real
our love will find a way.
Just like the ocean finds its way to shore
time and time again.
Our love dances and climbs in the sky
as it waits for time to pass us by.
When and if it returns,
maybe we'll be a little more wise
and a little less young.
but our hearts will still be the same
as they were that night,
and our souls will still be made up
of the same wild light.

Hell of a Man

You would fly me high
and get me to dance in the sky.
You made everything okay.
You were the light to my darkness.
You made me bright.
You made me better.
Now you're gone.
I still think of you, everyday, all the time.
We deserved a better goodbye.
Things weren't meant to be like this.
It was supposed to be you and I.
You still wander my mind.
You're someone else's angel now.
I hope you remember our last kiss,
because that might be our last goodbye.
I really hope it's not.

The Man I Love

Some time ago I was alone,
my life laced in black and white.
Not much mattered.
Then you came into it and showed me
what it was like to be loved.
Now I'm alone again.
It's worse than it was before.
Because you not only filled my void,
you consumed it.
What was empty, then filled,
is more empty than before.
Instead of my heart being behind my ribcage
it ran to you, because it loves you so much.
I'm trying my hardest to pick myself up.
It's a battle I fight everyday.
I try to remind myself that I'm lucky
to have felt the kind of love
that brings this kind of heartbreak.
I continue loving you despite this pain

Currently and Always You

I still remember the galaxies in your eyes
and the stardust in your heart.
I think of them quite often
as I wonder about you.
Oh my love,
you have me wrapped around your finger
even still.
You left me wondering
if everything were a waste of time,
if it meant anything to you as it did to me.
I often think of how things were
and imagine them as if they are the present.
Despite my heart no longer being in my body,
I can still feel my affection for you.
I miss you.
I only wish you felt the same.

Poems I Write

I write these poems and give them to the world.
I wonder how many eyes read over my words
and think of the one they cherish.
While they do I am left alone,
with ink covered fingers holding a secret.
Would you like to know what it is?
I write poems about you,
as well as vent to the stars.
They see me - broken.
They smile and say,
"You are the moon my dear,
and he is the sun.
Forever etched in one another."

I'm Still Here

My pieces are all around me.
I pick myself up,
and attempt to glue myself back together.
I'm missing my heart,
but I know it's safe with you.
I'm broken in a million ways.
Years and years of being torn apart
and left alone.
Days and nights spent wishing for something.
People continuously breaking me,
but they broke the wrong parts of me.
They forgot that broken people grow wings,
so they can learn to fly.

My Wish to the Stars

I remember long ago, every night,
I'd wish to be with you more often.
It's midnight somewhere.
Maybe it's here.
I have a wish:
sunkissed hair,
ocean blue eyes,
wild heart,
a peaceful soul,
and skin that's climbed the giants.
I wish for you.
Every day. Every night.

Constellation Messages

Not many people know
the type of love I have for you.
It's as pure,
as the mountains you climb
and the ink stained on my fingertips.
It's as epic as the look we share,
as I stare into the deep sea of your eyes
and you into the rich chocolate of mine.
It's as raw,
as the peaches and honey
that drip from our lips.
but for a short while,
you were the reason I believed love was pain.
Sometimes I'd wish
for the memories of you to disappear.
but instead
I lock them away in my mind and my heart.
Where no one can see but me.
Is love pain? I ask you.
Or did the stars cross us forever
and give us the wrong time?
Forever I'll love you mi amor.
Even from afar.
Even though we're apart now,
we're lucky to have experienced
that liquid sunshine type of passion.
Not many get to.
So remember me, my sunshine,
whenever you look into the sky

and see the stars.
Wherever we are in the future
we'll be looking at the sky
and I'll whisper a message for you
to the constellations,
"As you wish."

Patient

I want a love that consumes me,
but calms me to my core.
I want passion and adventure.
Someone to stay by my side.
Someone to love me wild.
Is that so wrong?
For me to want someone to stay
through the night till the morning
and even after.
You gave me that,
without an inkling of knowledge
of what I wanted.
Until my hope disappears,
I patiently wait for you to come back to me.

Only Us

Sometimes magic comes in different forms.
Like in the flap of butterfly wings,
or the beat of a hummingbird heart.
Like the mountains you climb on,
or the stroke of a pen.
Maybe even a smile or a laugh.
Maybe a kiss.
The purest magic can be found in, love.
Sometimes magic can hide for awhile,
but it never goes away.
It waits in space, because it is patient.
It disappears to give you a chance
to see the spark without its help.
If you find it, it comes back in full force.
You and I may be just small stars
of that never ending sky.
I know the light
that the earth brings to your sea blue eyes.
You know the sugar sweetness
that makes my lips turn up as I dance.
We're both made of stardust, dreams,
and memories.
The memories I'll cherish
and the dreams I'll hope come true.
Sometimes magic is two people in love,
it will go away, only to find them again.
Even if it doesn't come back
you and I know what you and I are.
Magic.

Stolen Heart

You stole my ice cold heart
and melted it.
You filled it,
with peaches and honey.
Soft and sweet.
You stole a poet's heart.
The ink stained words etched there
are inscribed into the stars.
You stole it
and now I give it to you.
You're the kind of person
I could write about till the end of my days.
We're etched into one another.
Forever.
Here I will write about you and our love.
That way our love can never die;
because it will live in the sky,
my heart,
and in these pages.

Until We Meet Again

Perhaps it's time to let you go.
Not because I want to,
but because life has gotten in the way.
Can I ever really let you go?
"No." my heart says.
"You hold onto him, the pain will numb itself
after a while, you won't stop loving him.
You'll just learn to cope."
Maybe you and I were meant to part ways
only so that we can find each other again.
You may think
this is me surrendering my will to fight,
but I assure you it is not.
I'm going to continue to fight like hell for you.
You may think
this is me saying goodbye,
but I assure you it is not.
We'll meet again, later in life.
It hurts like hell right now.
Perhaps it always will.
I long, for the day we meet again.
For the first time.

Till Death Do Us Part
I don't know what happens after death.
If there's a paradise
or if there's another life afterwards.
but if there is a next life
then what I do know is that
I will love you,
from this life to the next.
and if we don't meet in the next life
then I will still love you to the next one,
and the next, and the next.
I will love you to the ends of everything and on.

Epic Love

I want to be mad at you
for causing me this pain,
but I can't.
Because underneath all
of that confusion and suffering,
I love you.
You forever changed me.
You helped heal me.
I will forever cherish you.
I will always love you,
but it's time to let you go.
For me, for you, for us.
Maybe one day I'll see you again, and we'll smile.
Because we'll think back to that year we shared,
and we'll know that we healed,
and that it was epic.

Forever in My Heart,
but it's Time to Let You Go

I've changed, again.
You changed me, again.
Or maybe this time, it was me.
I've been waiting for you
to realize it was a mistake;
that you miss me, love me.
I've been in so much pain, waiting for that day.
It's time to let you go, completely.
I'll shed my skin like a snake.
I'm not saying I don't love you.
It's that I do.
Maybe we'll meet again later in life,
but if not, that's alright.
Because I know that we were magic.
My heart will always belong to you.
I thank you for everything.
You brought me peace
and showed me how to love.
I'll appreciate you always.
I don't want to say goodbye
because that means forever.
So for now I say,
"Until we meet again;"

I Hope
The moving pictures
course through my head in waves.
The ocean blue of your eyes haunt me
reminding me of what I lost.
The process of healing
has made me realize
that I will always love you.
I hope I'll make you proud.

One More Time

My hummingbird heart beats for you.
My hidden butterflies
fly crazily for you.
Every atom inside me
is buzzing.
Instead of being in chaos
everything is in harmony.
They say that you know you're in love
when everything inside you is calm,
like everything makes sense.
I often wonder if you think of me
as I do you.
It's always been you.
Our souls collide just right.
but here we are,
back where we started.
As strangers.
Look into my cosmic eyes my dear
as I gaze into yours.
Lets not start over,
but let us grow
and learn from one another once more.

What Poets Look For

Some poets look for love,
so that they can write.
Some poets look for heartbreak,
so that they can write.
They look for the heart as well as the soul
to put into words.
I look for you,
so that I can write.
I see you through the eyes of my younger self,
the one who was in love with you.
I see you through the eyes of my present self,
the one who just so happens to still
be in love with you.
I've written poems about you in this journal
and I continue to do so,
despite you being so far away.
I'll keep a few blank pages,
in case you come back.

Cosmic Love

They ask me about love
and when they do I think of you.
I don't know how to talk about it
without thinking of your ocean eyes.
I'm dancing in the cosmos,
you're climbing up the mountains.
I miss you.
I know that you can't love someone
into loving you,
but you can stop playing it safe and take a risk.
You can tell them that you love them.
Just as I am telling you.
So my angel,
when you reach the top of those mountains
and you make your way to the stars.
Come find me within the cosmos.
I'll be waiting for you there.

Therapeutic Sessions With the Stars

I ask the stars for guidance.
I ask them,
"Can someone still be completely in love
with another after so much time has passed?"
The stars replied shimmering,
"As you look into his ocean eyes
you'll see that the answer is, yes."
I know that we were real.
I can feel it in every atom of my body.
Let's take a chance.
It isn't too late for us.
It isn't too late.
Come dance with me
under the moonlight.
As we learn to grow again.
Together.

Heart Laid Down

I have stone cold walls around myself,
but you've always been able to see
right through them.
As if they were transparent.
I knew then, that you'd forever be my always.
Loving you was never a part of my plan.
In between
laughing,
dancing,
and smoking a blunt
I fell head over heels
for the boy with golden hair.
I know you might be scared of my heart;
of the unknown,
but it's tearing me apart.
You not knowing.
So here it is.
Here is my ink stained heart
covering these pages.
For you.
This is what I can offer you.
I've laid down my cards.
Now my dear,
I'm looking into those ocean eyes.
The ones that reflect the stars.
Waiting for you to grab my hand
and take a chance.
With me
and my heart.

Infiniteness of It All

This love of ours has traveled
through honey and pain.
I've recorded it
with ink stained words and shades of paint.
We've seen it on
ferris wheels and on the side of mountains.
In the huge vastness of our lives
I know that we were
complete and utter magic.
Liquid sunshine.
Raw and pure.
Just like peace and peaches.

Fear

They say that what you're most afraid
to write, write that.
but I'm not afraid of what I feel for you.
I'm not afraid
of what you'll say when we meet again.
I'm not afraid
of you never falling in love with me again.
What I'm afraid of is you forgetting.
Forgetting me, our love, and the magic.
I don't want to be a forgotten memory
lost to the wind.
Because I will never forget you, ever.
I'll keep you close to my heart and soul,
never forgetting.
When everything else turns to dust,
I'll remember you.

Risk

We're young
with the world in our grasp.
As we've come to learn, life is short.
So here I am.
At the edge of a cliff.
Here I am taking a risk, here I am before you.
Wearing my heart on my sleeve.
I've laid down my cards for you to see.
Mistakes were made.
Time has passed,
but I am once again the sweet warm air
that runs down the canyon at night.
I am still the same woman
who loves you with everything she has.
Now I can't promise everything will work out,
but I can love you everyday.
For the rest of our lives and even after.
I'll never leave you.
Take my hand my love.
Don't be afraid to take this chance.
Won't you take this risk with me?
If my words find you,
and you'd like to take my hand.
Find me.

A Little Girls First

You, dad, were supposed to be my first love,
but instead you were my first heartbreak.
You, my sunshine, were my first and only love,
and my worst heartbreak.
All the fairytale books say
a girls first love is a man,
but it should be a woman instead.
I should have been my first love.

Her Constant

There's always two sounds around her.
The click clack of a keyboard
or the scribble of a pen.
She writes and writes and writes.
What is it all about? They ask.
She answers the simplest way she knows how,

"A rock climber
who gifted me the world
within wildflowers."

My Flower Boy
Once, so full and lush.
Once, so young and naive.
but they start to fade.
Are we not all a part
of the crowded wilting garden?
Falling and dying, losing our beauty and youth.
We don't think we'll bloom again.
>You smell like sunshine and wild flowers.
>You don't pick them to pointlessly
>kill them, you give them to your flower girl.
>>When I saw them on that window sill
>>I fell in love with you,
>>my wild flower boy.

The lush petals will wilt and fall,
they'll become paper thin.
>>>but every time I close my eyes
>>>all I see is you
>>>looking me in the eye,
>>>standing outside my window,
>>>as you whisper *"I love you."*
>>>Even though you're not here,
>>>I remember those wild flowers
>>>everyday.
>They've frayed,
>but look, here they are.
>*Lasting*, in my heart all this time

Are we not all a part of the crowded garden?
Wilting, growing, blooming.
Knowing we'll bloom again.

If the Stars Can, I Can

I broke your heart a year ago,
and you shattered mine.
I was holding on to you too tight
that you slipped through my fingers.
I should've known better
than to try to hold you down,
you were meant to fly.
Those wings of yours
constantly fly you to me within my dreams
and I wake up more in love with you than
yesterday, but you're not here.
I envy the ones who came into your life
around the same time I did.
They got to stay with you
while I'm across the cosmos.
I'd walk across the world,
swim in every ocean,
cross every river,
travel to the ends of the universe
if it meant you'd be there.
Instead I do the very thing the stars do for you,
I wait for you to come back to me.

Our Poetic Beginning

It all began behind a grocery store,
with a girl and a boy.
It started with wild flowers on window sills
and midnight kisses under the night sky.
Two kids in love. Two souls entwined.
I never sought out perfection,
but that's what you are to me.
Perfectly imperfect.
Was our love a once in a lifetime experience?
No, I don't believe that.
I don't believe we met for no reason,
I don't believe we fell in love
like we did for no reason.
I know that the constellations will lead us
back to each other one day.
There's something to be said about a love
like that, the type of connection that leads
the two lovers back to each other.
Could it be that I'm wrong?
No, otherwise our beginning
wouldn't have been so poetic to begin with.
Maybe our love was chaos and magic,
in their purest forms.
Our love was one of the greatest
the stars have ever seen.

Still in Love
I've been in love only once.
It was the type of love
people look for their entire lives.
I had found it in a young man's ocean eyes.
I never said the words and meant them,
until I met him.
Until I met you.
I don't think I could've said them
to anybody else, but you.
I feel like I can say anything to you,
even now.

Two Parts of a Whole

We're minuscule,
two — of many in this universe.
and yet, we met.
In the vastness of space and time, in a moment.
We fell from the clouds,
but instead of crashing down
we flew into one another.
We collided.
Our hearts saw who we were
before our eyes even understood.
Two kinds of stardust, one star.
Two parts of a whole.
Never belonging to each other,
belonging together.
Its magic,
it's something that never happens every day.
In the eb and flow of everything and anything.
We never looked away.
I couldn't stay, but I could never look away.
It was you then, it's you still.
Will you look my way once more?
We aren't kids anymore,
then again that's what we always said.
So magic shouldn't exist any longer,
but when our eyes lock that's all there is.
Magic.
Take my hand, kiss my lips, spin me around,
let's climb up to the clouds.
Come home with me as the sun rises and sets.

Dance with me and let's see where this goes.
I will never look away.
I wish I had found these words
back when we were kids,
so that time wouldn't have been wasted
on our growth.
However, the bigger the star
the brighter it shines.

All the Possibilities

They say time heals all pain,
but we've learned that life is short
and that time is a lie.
It's been so long now
and I can still feel the heartbreak
like it was yesterday.
Our memories are packed in boxes
sitting near the door,
waiting to be reopened again.
Miles and miles away from one another,
but I'm still holding onto hope.
As life is short all we have are memories,
take a risk with me
and let's make more of them together.
If you take a chance on me,
there's a great possibility
it'll turn out better than alright.
I love you knowing
that you loving me back is uncertain,
but I'm willing to take that possibility.

Completely Bonkers

Perhaps I've gone mad.
Maybe I'm just a hopeless romantic.
Perhaps I'm just a girl in love.
I've written and written to the point my love
for you is now inscribed into countless pages.
The thick inked words
have slipped through my heart and
onto parchment.
This book that I once carried within me
is now out in the universe.
Maybe, I have indeed gone a bit mad.
I've got it in my head
that once the book is completed,
it would travel the world to find you.
and bring you back to me.
I've gone mad with hope and love.

Rose

He fell in love with me, a poet.
Do you know what that's like?
It's orgasmic and sensual,
but beware of what you might see
when you look into a poet's mind full of words.
For it is dark and gut-wrenching,
but if you look a little harder you'll see
that it's light and sweet, gentle.
He fell in love with the flower and the thorns.

Vulnerability

At times I'd be angry or sad.
Sometimes the storm within me
would come to the surface.
I tried so hard to hide it from you,
I didn't want you to see.
You never tried to tear my walls down,
but you always saw right through me,
you saw me.
When I realized that,
I explained to you my thorn-like past.
I told you that I wouldn't always be easy,
that you might have to be patient
while I pull myself from my weeded mind.
I told you that it became a habit of mine
to apologize for the mess I was.
Every time I was angry or sad,
every time I was caught up in my own mind,
you looked at me
in a way no one had ever looked at me.
You made me raw, vulnerable.
With that look you listened,
you understood,
you loved.
I'm still not easy, but I've changed.
You taught me that it's okay
to be vulnerable,
to be open.
Every time you looked at me like that,

it was enough reason to pull myself
out of the dark.
No one has ever looked at me quite like that.

Again

It's 12:01am, the start of a new day.
Parts of us taken by yesterday,
new ones born today.
I look up at the moon, she's full tonight.
I look at it, knowing somewhere
wherever you are, you see it too.
The crickets sing their song
while I quickly scribble down these words.
I pull out the photo that has become
my bookmark, it's of you.
I miss you,
just like I have everyday for over a year.
I know my message will reach you,
the stars told me so.
but I don't know what you'll say,
if you'll take my hand or say goodbye.
Whatever you do,
I'll continue to look at that photo everyday.
Whether I look at the glossy paper
or you with bedhead when I wake.
For me, it'll always be you.
Oh my sunshine, let me come back home.
Let us find home, again, in each other.
Let's find each other, again.

The Search

We've let go, but maybe we haven't.
Maybe our forever was small,
or maybe it was only the beginning.
When I think about our love versus
our mistakes and heartbreaks;
those flaws seem so small to me in my mind.
So much separates us, including us.
We're strangers again, but we don't have to be.
We had our little forever
and maybe once was enough.
Or maybe it wasn't even close.
I know nothing is forever,
even you and me.
I also know everything is eternal,
even you and me.
We can find our little forever again,
if you'll help me look for it.
I know you're hesitant in a search like this,
but you'll never know
if you don't ever try again.
So lets try.

What Is Love?

The way you looked at me that day and everyday
can only be described as a man
who is utterly and completely in love
with the woman in front of him.
It was soft like the mini waves
of the ocean on the shore.
Many spend their entire lives
trying to define what love is.
I found the answer to that
behind a grocery store,
but more so from miles away
from the person I learned it from.
Love is the small glimmer I see in your eyes
as you look at me,
it's the smile you make
when you think I'm not paying attention,
it's the feeling of freedom and security,
it's the flap of butterfly wings
as it leaves your finger,
it's watching you climb up and up and up,
it's seeing you after we were no longer together
only to find each other again,
it's being half way across the country for a year
only to still be completely in love with you.
All I want is to see you happy
even if it's without me.
That's love.

The Book pt 1

I quit this dream of mine.
You brought it back to life
by being my inspiration.
I never thought I'd finish it,
but something has changed within my heart.
It says,
"You have finally completed the book."
There's a peace to that.
Oh my sunshine,
my love for you that consumes me
is still raging in the flames of us.
When the stars whispered our names
behind that grocery store;
You became my new dream.
A dream that became my reality,
and now once more a dream.
Oh the dream-makers and all of the stars
shout at us,
"Just be together already!"
as we continually find each other.
So when you're ready for me,
I'll be ready for you.
Because my love,
this dream I will never quit.

New Beginnings

A new chapter is beginning.
For the both of us.
We flipped the page.
I wonder where we are now.
Things didn't turn out like we planned.
Now we're gonna cry alone.
Each of us up on our own throne.
Wishing and hoping that you'll turn back.
So maybe you're thinking of me now:
With a blunt in one hand
and my book in the other.
As you're reading my words
that little part of me
that's in your heart is making you smile.
It's such a fine smile.
Know that feeling is deja vu.
You're feeling me write this to you.

The Book pt 2

Perhaps this chapter is over.

This prose is one of the last.

This book is finished.

Our chapter over,

but not our story.

Not even close.

There will always be more to write.

Maybe it'll be for you.

Maybe it'll be for me.

One things for sure,

we will be okay.

A,B,C,D
The thick dipped words
cover her body like tattoos.
The poems in her heart and soul
are waiting to be written.
The alphabet playing in her mind like music.
Her world has ended before, multiple times,
and when it did she closed the book.
Her world restarted each morning she woke.
This time her world did not end,
but she did end the story.
She began carving her own path
into her new beginning.
She could finally fly
and started to make her own choices.
She let go of her past
and for the second time of her life,
she felt free.

- Adulthood

How Do I Learn How to Say Goodbye?
So many have left, while others have stayed.
but how do you know
when it's your turn to walk away?
Sometimes these words are temporary
and other times it means forever.
My father left so long ago,
but he never taught me how to say goodbye.
Friends came and went,
but they never taught me how to say goodbye.
The elderly have lived and died,
but they never taught me how to say goodbye.
All those people that left and I don't know how.
Someone teach me how to say goodbye.
I don't want to say the words -
but I'm grown now and it's my turn to fly.
I love you Mom, forever and a day.
I don't want to say the words -
but I hope we'll find each other one last time.
I love you my sunshine, forever and a day.
Someone teach me how to say goodbye.

Sugar

I don't know who you are anymore
and you don't know me either,
but we know each other's souls by heart.
That's the part we're in love with,
no matter how much we change.
If we find each other in the future
maybe we'll read this book
and remember when we fell in love.
We'll remember the magic.
We'll look back at our broken hearts
and stupid mistakes that have gotten us
to where we are,
and it will be worth all the pain.
If not, then you'll read this book
and remember the girl that tasted like sugar,
who became the woman
that inscribed your love
into the stars and into these pages.
You'll remember me,
and I will love you
forever and ever.

To C.B

I wrote this for you,
I need you to understand that this is all for you.
Everyone that reads my words
will think of their special someone,
but this is for you.
You're the only one
who will truly comprehend this.
No one else will really understand.
In the beginning I said I'd never fall in love,
because I was scared of getting hurt.
That night though,
it was late and we were dancing
and laughing way too damn hard.
I couldn't help it, I fell in love with you.
This didn't happen the way we wanted
or the way it was supposed to,
but this was more real than most things.
It was magic. It was epic.
I've tried to write what you taught me,
what we saw, and everything I felt.
but some things are meant
to only stay in our hearts.
For us and us alone.
I hope one day we find each other again.
Until then. . .
Forever I love you. Always I miss you;

- Your Flower Girl

xx

About the Book

Forever Etched In Me is a collection of poetry
about the highs and lows of young love.
It'll take you to the peaks of mountains,
and ask you to dance in fields of flowers.
It's raw and sweet,
just like the sticky sweetness
of peaches and honey on his lips.
It's my heart engraving itself into these pages,
for him, and the stars.

CPSIA information can be obtained
at www.ICGtesting.com
Printed in the USA
LVHW082306050920
665202LV00008B/16